The Secret Life of the
Sea Otter

Laurence Pringle

Illustrated by
Kate Garchinsky

ASTRA YOUNG READERS

AN IMPRINT OF ASTRA BOOKS FOR YOUNG READERS

New York

Lutris takes a nap.

She has been busy all morning, diving underwater to hunt for food. Now she covers her eyes with her paws to shut out the light, and falls asleep. Ocean waves rock her gently in her water bed.

Lutris floats easily among saltwater plants called *giant kelp* that grow near the rocky seashore. Other sea otters swim or float nearby. Like Lutris, they are all female southern, or California, sea otters, gathered in a group called a *raft*. Some are mothers, taking care of their pups.

Lutris's world is shared with other animals. Sometimes harbor seals and sea lions swim past, or rest on rocks. Gulls, cormorants, and pelicans fly overhead.

When Lutris wakes from her nap, she grooms her fur. Sea otters have the thickest fur of all *mammals*. It helps keep them warm in the cold water of the northern Pacific Ocean.

Sea otters have very flexible *spines* (backbones), so Lutris can twist and turn to reach all over her body to brush her fur with her sharp claws. This grooming traps tiny air bubbles between the hairs. Sometimes Lutris even blows air into her fur coat. All that air helps her float, and also helps keep her warm.

Lutris also protects herself from cold by floating on her back and raising her head and all four feet out of the chilly water.

Her grooming all done, Lutris floats in the sun—but now she is hungry. She flips over and dives down, down, down into the secret watery world of the kelp forest, where these plants hold fast to the seafloor.

Kelp is a *habitat* of many *sea* creatures. Fish, squid, octopuses, crabs, snails, clams, mussels, *sea stars*, and *sea urchins* live there. Since Lutris is a *predator*, she has favorite animals to eat (*prey*). So do other otters that hunt in the kelp forest. Usually there is plenty of food for all.

Lutris kicks her strong back legs. She has skin between the toes of her big back feet, so they work like powerful paddles or flippers. Sometimes she swishes her tail back and forth. This also helps to push her through the water.

Lutris can see well underwater, but deep in the kelp forest it is very dark. She relies more on her sense of touch, using her bushy whiskers and the paws on her front feet to feel for food.

Lutris has been underwater, holding her breath, for more than two minutes. Now she swims up, up, up to the surface to breathe, and then to eat the food she gathered.

First she takes a flat stone from under her arm and places it on her chest. Then she grabs a clam with both front paws and bangs it again and again on the stone. The clamshell breaks. Lutris eats the clam that was hidden inside. She does the same with the other clam and the sea urchin she caught.

The stone she uses is a vital tool. Lutris tucks it away to use another time.
Then she rolls over so the clamshells and other leftovers are washed off her body.
Gulls hover above. They may swoop down to pluck a clam morsel from the water.

Energy from her food helps keep Lutris warm. She hunts both day and night. Underwater, she sometimes tugs on a mussel shell with both front paws, pulling it free from a rock. Or she grabs a crab. Or she finds a big *shellfish* called an *abalone*, then hits it with a stone to knock it loose. Each time she swims up to the surface, eager to eat her catch..

SCREECH! Near Lutris an otter calls out, then dives out of sight. It had seen the *dorsal fin* of a big shark slicing through the water.

In an instant, every otter dives to hide in the kelp forest below. The great white shark patrols along the edge of the kelp plants, then swims away. Sharks do sometimes catch otters, but they prefer to eat seals and sea lions, which have tasty fat called *blubber* in their bodies. Otters have no blubber.

Later, Lutris and the other otters pop to the surface. They watch warily to make sure that the shark is gone.

Day and night, Lutris eats and eats. She has been extra hungry because a baby was growing inside her body. Today her pup is born!

Lutris hugs her daughter to her chest. She coos and grunts as the pup nurses its first meal of milk. It was born with a special dense, fluffy fur coat that helps it float in the water. Lutris licks her baby's fur clean, then brushes it with her paws.

The newborn otter cannot swim or dive to hunt for food. Only her mother's warm, nutritious milk keeps her alive and healthy. But Lutris needs to hunt for food. Dozens of times each day and night, she must leave her daughter alone.

Lutris tries to keep her pup safe. Before she leaves to hunt, she often wraps a strand of kelp around her pup, to hold her in place. Then she dives underwater.

The pup gives a piping cry—a sea otter signal that means, "I'm here, I'm here." *Splash!* Lutris quickly returns, rolls onto her back, and snuggles her pup to her chest.

The baby otter begins to learn about her world at the ocean's edge. She feels and hears the rhythm of *undulating* waves. She hears the cries of gulls, and the squeals, grunts, and growls of otters. She also hears *tap, tap, tap, tap,* as her mother and nearby otters use their stone tools to crack open clams and other food.

She watches Lutris and tries to imitate what she sees. She learns to use her front paws to brush her own fur. She begins to swim a little on the surface.

As the pup grows, her fluffy baby fur is replaced with the short, dense fur coat she will have for life. Soon she learns to hold her breath and dive underwater. She becomes a strong swimmer and goes to play with other frisky young otters. They wrestle, chase, and roll over in the water.

Although the pup still likes the taste and comfort of her mother's milk, she begins to eat morsels of clam, crab, and other food that Lutris gives her. The pup will eat solid food and drink milk until she is six months old. Then she is *weaned*, no longer nursing milk.

The watery home of the otters is sometimes lit by sunbeams, or by stars, or hidden by dense fog. The otters feel gentle waves and also rough surf. And sometimes a fierce storm brings towering, dangerous waves.

Today's storm is like a monster, with winds that howl and waves that growl and roar. Mother otters and their pups cling to kelp and to one another.

Some kelp plants are ripped from the seafloor. Some pups are
swept away. They and their mothers scream loudly back and forth,
so the pups can be found and saved.

Lutris and her daughter hold tight and wait out the storm.

Weeks have passed. On this foggy day, the sea is calm. Now five months old, the otter pup has grown a lot. She is almost as big as her mother. Diving underwater with Lutris, she has learned how to find and gather food. And—*tap, tap, tap, tap*—she knows how to use a stone tool to open clams and mussels.

In a few more weeks, the young otter will be ready to swim off on her own. Now, though, she and Lutris may still hunt, eat, and rest together. Sometimes they both take a nap, rocked to sleep by gentle waves in their water bed.

More About Sea Otters

In this book, the sea otter is called Lutris because of the species' scientific name: *Enhydra lutris*. In Latin, *Lutris* means "otter," and from the Greek, *enhydra* means "living in water." Lutris of this book is a California or southern sea otter, one of three sea otter subspecies: southern (of central and southern California); northern (of the Aleutian Islands, Alaska, western Canada, and the states of Washington and Oregon); and Asian (of Japan and Russia). There are some small differences between these subspecies. The shapes of their skulls differ a bit. Also, northern sea otters eat some fish; their southern relatives rarely do.

Sea otters are in the weasel family, related to badgers, ferrets, fishers, martens, mink, weasels, and wolverines. Their closest relatives are river otters, which live in freshwater streams and ponds. Worldwide, there are twelve different species of river otters. Most kinds of river otters travel easily on land, and can catch some of their food there.

In contrast, sea otters seldom come ashore. Their flipper-like back feet are great for swimming, but make the otters move awkwardly on land. They eat, sleep, mate, give birth, and feed their young in water.

In addition to having unusual rear feet, sea otters are wonderfully adapted for their aquatic life in other ways. For example, a sea otter's ears fold down tightly when it dives. Its nostrils also shut. These quick actions keep water out of its ears and nose. Sea otters also have unusually large lungs and can stay underwater without breathing for more than five minutes. They can dive as deep as 250 feet, but usually find food in more shallow water, less than 50 feet down.

Sea otter pups are born with a full set of thirty-two teeth. Since otters eat mostly hard-shelled animals, they need especially tough teeth. Big molars in the back of their jaws can crack hard shells. Sharp cutting teeth in their lower jaws help otters grab and pull clams, mussels, and other foods from within their broken shells. So do the otters' nimble front paws.

To survive in the cold waters of the northern Pacific, sea otters digest food quickly to get warmth and energy. Since they lack the insulation of a layer of fat (blubber), sea otters get warmth by eating as much as one quarter of their own body weight every day. If a 100-pound human had the same need, that person would have to eat 25 pounds of food daily!

Sea otters can also thrive in cold water because of their two fur coats. The visible top part is made of long guard hairs. Beneath that is short, very dense underfur. It is many times more dense than the fur of other mammals. Dogs, for example, can have as many as 60,000 hairs per square inch of skin. Sea otters can have at least 650,000 hairs per square inch. As long as a sea otter keeps its fur well groomed, this incredibly dense fur keeps cold water from ever reaching its skin.

The unique fur of sea otters almost led to extinction of this species. Until the 1700s, sea otters thrived along many coasts of the North Pacific. This area, called the Pacific Rim, includes islands near Japan and Russia, the Aleutian Islands, and the North American coast, from Alaska to Mexico. In the 1740s, Russian explorers began hunting sea otters to sell their fur. The fine, dense otter fur could be made into coat collars, coats, and other clothing. It became a popular luxury. Eventually, the otters were hunted throughout their whole range. Since they lived close to shore and were often in sight on the surface, they were easily found and killed.

By the year 1900, sea otters were scarce or totally wiped out in many areas. They were saved from total extinction in 1911, when an international law stopped most otter hunting. By then, however, fewer than 2,000 sea otters remained in their once-vast range. For many years, people thought that no southern sea otters existed. Then, in 1938, a California rancher spotted a small raft of survivors.

Otter populations recovered slowly. One conservation effort that helped was restoring otters in places where they no longer lived. Between 1969 and 1972, for example, eighty-nine otters were captured alive off the Alaska coast and released by Vancouver Island, in British Columbia, Canada. Now more than 3,000 sea otters live there.

Many people love the ways that sea otters look and behave, but scientists discovered a different reason to treasure them: they are a *keystone species*. They are sometimes called "keepers of the kelp," and here is why. Sea urchins are a favorite sea otter food. When otters are scarce or absent, the number of sea urchins grows quickly. They feed on kelp plants and can eat so much they create an "urchin barren." The kelp forest and all the creatures that thrived in it are gone—simply because the otters are missing.

Kelp forests are also prized by humans because the tops of these plants are harvested, dried, and turned into a powder that is used in many products (including toothpaste, juices, and salad dressings). People in the kelp business are fond of sea otters. On the other hand, some people who harvest and sell clams, abalone, and sea urchins feel that plentiful sea otters hurt their business.

Even though sea otters recovered from near extinction, they still face many dangers. An oil spill from a ship just offshore can be deadly because otters can't clean this pollutant from their fur. Oil from a 1989 spill in Alaska's Prince William Sound killed several thousand sea otters.

Some otters die from disease or polluted water. Beginning in the 1990s, scientists learned about a new threat to otters. Near the Aleutian Islands, sea otters were being hunted and eaten by orcas (big dolphins that are also called killer whales). For countless years the two species had lived near each other peacefully. Why were orcas now attacking otters?

The answer, scientists found, came from a chain of changes. First, certain kinds of fish became scarce, perhaps because of overfishing by people, or warming ocean temperatures. These fish had been a main source of food for seals and sea lions. A lack of fish caused the numbers of seals and sea lions to drop. Orcas had always depended on seals and sea lions for much of their food. When their favorite prey became scarce, orcas began to hunt sea otters.

The recovery of sea otters from near extinction is a wonderful conservation success story. However, in the United States, the California sea otter is called an endangered species, and wherever sea otters live, they face old and new threats. Their survival depends on people working to protect them and their near-shore ocean habitat.

Glossary

Abalone: a large saltwater shellfish or mollusk whose soft, edible body is protected by a hard outer shell, like those of clams and mussels.

Blubber: a layer of fat beneath the skin of such saltwater mammals as seals, sea lions, and whales. Sea otters do not have this store of fat, so they must eat many pounds of food each day for warmth and energy.

Dorsal fin: the fin located on the back of many fishes, including sharks, and also on most whales and dolphins. When one of these animals swims close to the water surface, its dorsal fin can sometimes be seen poking up into the air.

Giant kelp: the largest seaweed and the largest saltwater algae plant. It grows in cold water and provides food and shelter for hundreds of marine animals.

Habitat: the natural home or environment where an animal or a plant lives.

Keystone species: an animal or plant species that is a vital part of a habitat or ecosystem, affecting many other species. Without its keystone species, an ecosystem may cease to exist. Sea otters enable kelp forests to thrive by eating many sea urchins. A lack of sea otters allows sea urchins to wipe out most kelp plants, and this removes the habitat for many other sea creatures whose lives depend on kelp.

Mammals: warm-blooded animals with hair or fur that give birth to live young. Female mammals feed their young with milk from mammary glands. Otters, bats, dogs, and humans are all mammals.

Predator: an animal whose main food is other animals that it kills.

Prey: an animal that is hunted for food by other animals.

Raft: a group of sea otters that stay close together while eating or resting. They sometimes hang on to seaweeds to avoid being carried away from their raft by currents or waves while asleep.

Shellfish: a water animal (not a fish) that is protected by a hard outer covering. Shellfish include clams, oysters, mussels, scallops, and also such crustaceans as crabs, shrimp, and lobsters.

Spine: a column of small backbones called vertebrae that support the body of a mammal, bird, reptile, amphibian, or fish. Animals that have no spines are called invertebrates. Worms, insects, and arachnids are invertebrates.

Undulating: a smooth rising-and-falling movement of water. The word "undulate" comes from a Latin word, *unda*, which means "wave." The whole body of an otter swimming underwater also undulates, in an up-and-down motion.

Weaned: the stage in the life of a young mammal when it no longer nurses milk from its mother.

More Books About Sea Otters

Brust, Beth Wagner. *Sea Otters*. San Diego, CA: Zoobooks (Wildlife Education, Ltd.), 1993.

Eszterhas, Suzi. *Sea Otter Rescue*. Berkeley, CA: Owlkids Books, 2016.

León, Vicki. *A Raft of Sea Otters*. Parsippany, NJ: Silver Burdett Press, 1995.

Tatham, Betty. *Baby Sea Otter*. New York: Henry Holt, 2005.

For Jackson Laurence Kelehan, like a sea otter pup, curious and eager to learn. Welcome to our family, and to a life full of adventure, discovery, and love. —LP

For the one and only Emery, whose joyful spirit and pure cuteness can only be matched by a sea otter's. Love, Aunt Kate —KG

The author and illustrator thank Jessica Fujii, assistant manager, sea otter research, at California's Monterey Bay Aquarium, for her careful review of the text and illustrations.

The illustrator thanks photographers Tom and Pat Leeson for access to their extensive catalog of sea otter images.

Astra Young Readers
An imprint of Astra Books for Young Readers,
a division of Astra Publishing House
astrapublishinghouse.com
Printed in China

ISBN: 978-1-63592-325-4 (hc)
ISBN: 978-1-63592-571-5 (eBook)
Library of Congress Control Number: 2021906404

First edition
10 9 8 7 6 5 4 3 2

The text is set in Mercurius CT.
The illustrations are painted digitally in Procreate.

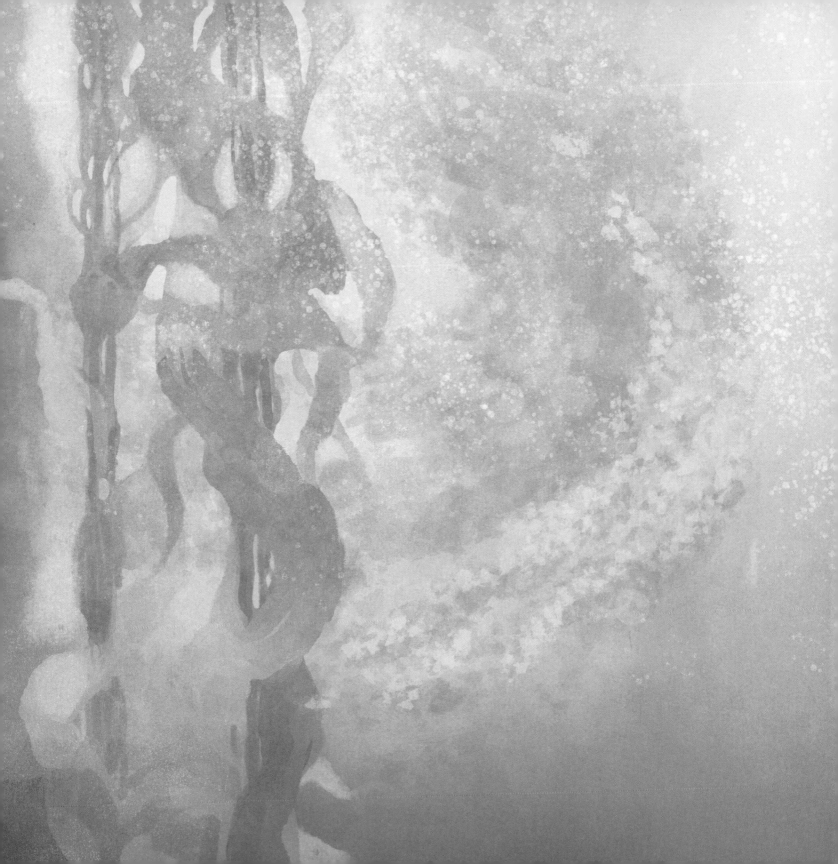